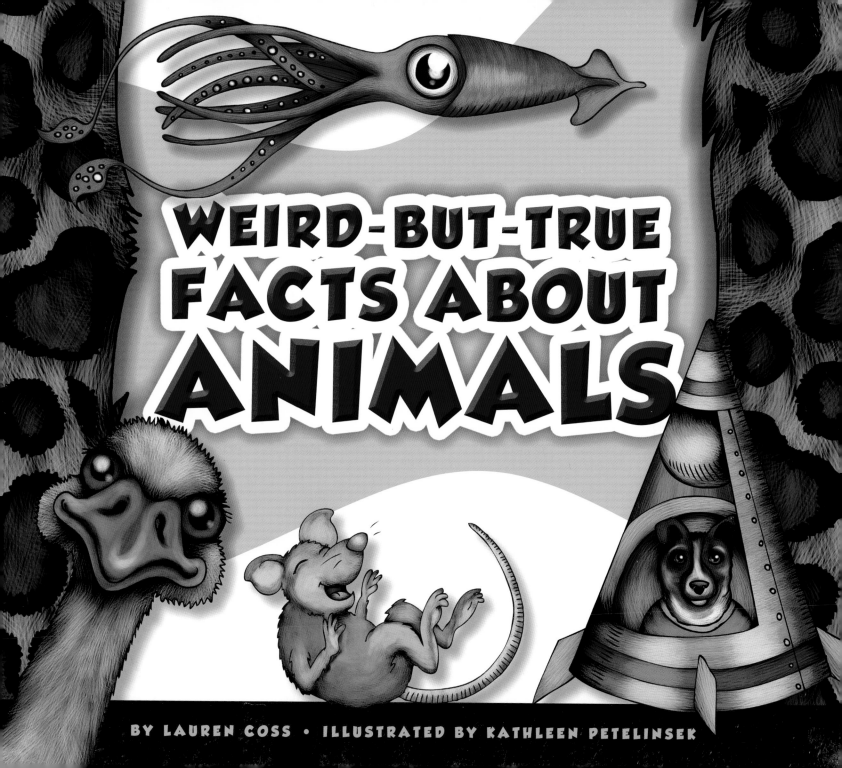

WEIRD-BUT-TRUE FACTS ABOUT ANIMALS

BY LAUREN COSS • ILLUSTRATED BY KATHLEEN PETELINSEK

The Child's World

Published by The Child's World®
1980 Lookout Drive • Mankato, MN 56003-1705
800-599-READ • www.childsworld.com

Acknowledgments
The Child's World®: Mary Berendes, Publishing Director
Red Line Editorial: Editorial direction
The Design Lab: Design
Amnet: Production

ISBN 9781614734123
LCCN 2012946519

Printed in the United States of America
Mankato, MN
November, 2012
PA02143

About the Author

Lauren Coss is a writer and editor who lives in Saint Paul, Minnesota. She loves learning new facts, and her favorite animal is her dog, Angel.

About the Illustrator

Kathleen Petelinsek loves to draw and paint. She lives next to a lake in southern Minnesota with her husband, Dale; two daughters, Leah and Anna; two dogs, Gary and Rex; and her fluffy cat, Emma.

TABLE OF CONTENTS

INTRODUCTION

The animal kingdom is an awesome place. Animals fly high in the skies and dig deep underground. They live in lake bottoms, caves, and the tops of trees. Some animals are so strange they might seem as if they are from another planet! Get ready to learn some fascinating facts about big and small animals across the globe. And remember, even though these facts may seem weird, they are all true!

WOOF!

ON FOUR LEGS

If you are in a Southeast Asian forest and smell buttery popcorn, it might be a binturong.

The binturong is a small **mammal** nicknamed the bearcat. It naturally smells like popcorn.

An aardvark's tongue can be up to 1 foot (.3 m) long.

Most aardvarks are about the size of a large pig, so that is an enormous tongue! They use it to lick termites out of their mounds.

A three-toed sloth only spends 10 percent of its life moving.

It spends the rest of its time sleeping in trees.

Tasmanian devils yawn when they are threatened.

But don't be fooled. They are actually one of the most aggressive mammals in the animal world.

The first living creature in space was a dog named Laika.

She was sent into orbit in 1957 after months of training.

A cow poops an average of 120 pounds (54.4 kg) every day.

That is as much as a small adult woman weighs.

Cheetahs can run more than 60 miles per hour (97 km/h).

They are the fastest land animal and can go from 0 to 60 miles per hour (97 km/h) in three seconds.

The star-nosed mole can smell underwater.

This strange-looking animal has a pink snout made up of 22 tentacles. The mole uses this unusual nose to blow bubbles underwater. When the bubbles touch a tasty creature, such as a small fish, the mole gets a whiff of it.

Rats are ticklish and laugh when they are tickled.

Scientists tickled rats and measured their responses. The rats made happy chirps as if they enjoyed the tickling. They even came back for more after the scientists stopped tickling them.

Koalas have fingerprints just like humans.

In fact, they are so similar, it is almost impossible to tell them apart from human fingerprints.

Coyotes and badgers often hunt as a team.

The coyote chases the prey above ground, and the badger follows the prey into a burrow. According to scientists, coyotes that hunt with a badger catch one-third more prey than coyotes hunting alone.

A lion's roar can be heard from 5 miles (8 km) away.

Lions are very **territorial**, and they use their powerful roar to warn off intruders that are getting too close.

There are more sheep than people in New Zealand.

With approximately 40.1 million sheep and 4.18 million people on the island, there are ten sheep per person.

Even though they live very far north, polar bears are more likely to overheat than to freeze.

Their bodies are very good at keeping in heat. Because of this, they would rather walk than run.

Porcupines float.

A porcupine's quills have a filling similar to a sponge that allows it to float in water.

Camels, cats, and polar bears have three eyelids.

Kangaroos have to hop everywhere because their legs cannot move separately.

They can hop up to 35 miles per hour (56 km/h).

WET AND WILD

A goldfish is only gold if it stays in the sunlight.

Goldfish have **pigmentation** just like humans. Without regular sunlight, they turn a shade of grayish white.

Seahorses have no stomachs.

This means they have to eat almost nonstop so they don't starve.

An octopus can squeeze through a space as small as its eye.

Octopuses have no skeletons, so they can form their bodies into narrow shapes. Octopuses are also very smart. This makes them great escape artists. In 2009, an octopus named Sid in a New Zealand aquarium learned how to open his tank and escaped. He spent five days hiding in a drainage system until a staff member found him. A month later, he was released into the ocean.

The pink handfish doesn't swim.

Instead, it walks along the ocean floor. This rare fish lives off the coast of Tasmania.

A shark's sense of smell is so sharp, it can sense one drop of blood in an Olympic-sized swimming pool.

These fish are amazing predators that have been around since the time of the dinosaurs.

Some lobsters are born bright blue.

This condition is very rare. Only one in every 4 million lobsters is born blue.

Tiny pistol shrimp are some of the loudest creatures in the sea.

Most pistol shrimp are less than 1 inch (2.5 cm) in length, but they make a noise louder than a gunshot. Each shrimp has one large claw, which it snaps shut when hunting. The snap creates a bubble, and the bursting bubble causes the noise—and enough pressure to stun nearby prey, such as small crabs.

Oysters change genders at least once during their lifetime.

Scientists think this is related to their environmental conditions. Young oysters are usually male. But in clean water with lots of food, a male oyster will change itself into a female so it can reproduce.

SMALL AND SLIMY

The purple frog spends most of its life buried up to 13 feet (4 m) underground.

It comes out only two weeks of every year to mate.

Cockroaches fart once every 15 minutes on average.

Snakes can't blink.

In fact, they don't even have eyelids. Instead, they have a clear covering that protects their eyes. When a snake sheds its skin, the eye cap turns cloudy or blue.

There are more than 1 million ants for every human on Earth.

The last animal in the dictionary is the zyzzyva.

It is a South American weevil, a type of beetle that eats plants and crops.

The mudpuppy is a salamander that barks like a dog.

This is the only salamander **species** that makes noise. Many people think it sounds like a barking dog.

In its lifetime, one worker bee produces just 1/12 of a teaspoon of honey.

In summer months, most worker bees live no longer than six weeks.

Banana slugs have 27,000 teeth.

Rats and mice are found on every continent except Antarctica.

However, they live on an island off the coast of Antarctica. Scientists think it is only a matter of time before they make it to the mainland.

Dragonflies cannot hear, smell, or taste.

However, their eyesight makes up for it. Dragonflies can see almost 360 degrees around them.

ON THE WING

Ostriches' eyes are bigger than their brains.

Butterflies taste with tiny sensors on their feet.

When a butterfly is getting ready to lay eggs, it lands on different plants to find out which would make good caterpillar food. If the plant tastes good, the butterfly might lay its eggs there.

Pigeons can always find their way home.

Scientists think they can sense Earth's magnetic field, helping them navigate. For centuries, people used homing pigeons to carry messages long distances. The pigeons could be transported great distances, but when they were released they would faithfully fly home.

They may be bloodsuckers, but vampire bats take care of their own.

The mammals have been known to help out other bats. A vampire bat will sometimes adopt an orphaned baby bat, caring for it as if it were the adult bat's own **offspring**.

23

Some birds can **migrate** more than 7,000 miles (11,000 km) without taking a break.

In 2007, scientists tracked a female godwit that flew from Alaska to New Zealand without stopping for food, water, or rest. The journey took the bird nine days.

Great-horned owls have long eyelashes.

Like human eyelashes, owls' eyelashes help protect their eyes.

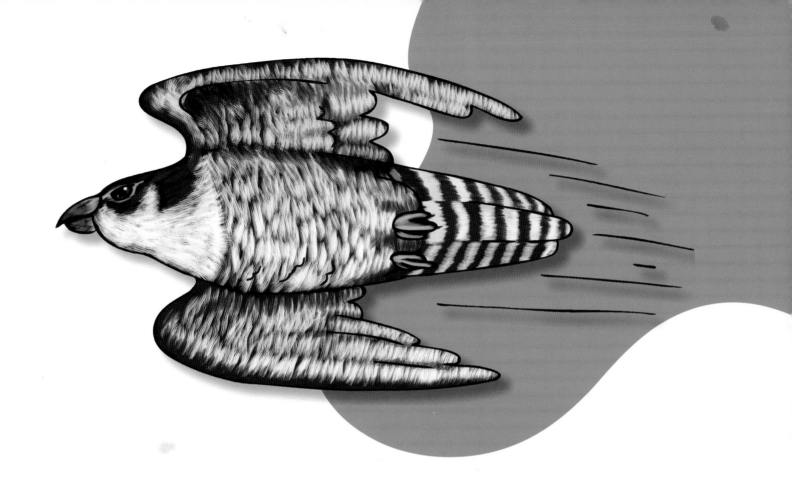

Peregrine falcons can fly more than 200 miles per hour (322 km/h).

That makes them the fastest animal on Earth on land, sea, or sky. These fast flyers can be found on every continent except Antarctica.

Only female mosquitoes bite humans.

Male mosquitoes eat nectar and plant juices.

LARGE AND SMALL

The growl of an elephant's stomach can be heard from a distance of almost two football fields away.

Blue whale babies grow fast.

A blue whale baby is called a calf. Drinking its mother's milk, a blue whale calf grows an average of 200 pounds (90.7 kg) a day for its first year of life.

A giant squid's eye can be as large as a beach ball.

The rest of the squid is large, too. The biggest squid ever found was 59 feet (18 m) long and weighed as much as a small car.

For humans, hippopotamuses are the most dangerous mammals in the world.

They kill more people each year than any other wild animal except mosquitoes. They also sweat an oily, red liquid that looks like blood, making them look even scarier. The oil helps protect their skin from the sun and germs and helps keep it from drying out.

The smallest mammal in the world is the bumblebee bat.

These tiny creatures live in Southeast Asia, and each one weighs only .07 ounces (2 grams). That is less than a nickel weighs.

It may be small, but the dung beetle can lift 1,141 times its own weight.

That makes it the world's strongest animal.

Some giant clams have been around since Abraham Lincoln was president.

Scientists believe some living giant clams are up to 150 years old. That makes them some of the oldest living creatures on Earth. These huge mollusks live up to their name. They can weigh more than 500 pounds (227 kg).

The world's smallest frog could sit on a dime.

The frog, which was recently discovered by scientists in the rainforests of New Guinea, is only .3 inches (.77 cm) long, about the size of a fly. It is the smallest known animal with a backbone.

GLOSSARY

mammal (MAM-ul)
A mammal is a warm-blooded animal with a spine that usually has hair and feeds its young with milk. Blue whales are the biggest mammals.

migrate (MYE-grate)
Animals that migrate move from one place to another, usually during different seasons. Many birds migrate to colder climates in the spring.

offspring (AWF-spring)
An offspring is an animal's young. A vampire bat might care for another bat's offspring.

pigmentation (pig-munt-TAY-shun)
Pigmentation is the natural coloring of an animal or plant. Goldfish and humans both have pigmentation.

species (SPEE-sheez)
Animals that are closely related to each other are part of the same species. Different salamanders in a species have different features.

territorial (ter-i-TOR-ee-ul)
A person or animal is territorial when they protect an area of land they consider their own. Lions are very territorial.

LEARN MORE

BOOKS

Aruego, Jose, and Ariane Dewey. *Weird Friends: Unlikely Allies in the Animal Kingdom*. New York: Harcourt, 2002.

Bailey, Jacqui. *Amazing Animal Facts*. New York: DK Children, 2003.

Burnie, David. *Amazing Animals Q & A*. New York: DK Publishing, 2007.

WEB SITES

Visit our Web site for links about weird animal facts:
childsworld.com/links

Note to Parents, Teachers, and Librarians: We routinely verify our Web links to make sure they are safe and active sites. So encourage your readers to check them out!

INDEX